This planner belongs to :

_____

2025

January

S	M	T	W	T	F	S
			1	2	3	4
5	6	7	8	9	10	11
12	13	14	15	16	17	18
19	20	21	22	23	24	25
26	27	28	29	30	31	

February

S	M	T	W	T	F	S
						1
2	3	4	5	6	7	8
9	10	11	12	13	14	15
16	17	18	19	20	21	22
23	24	25	26	27	28	

March

S	M	T	W	T	F	S
						1
2	3	4	5	6	7	8
9	10	11	12	13	14	15
16	17	18	19	20	21	22
23	24	25	26	27	28	29
30	31					

April

S	M	T	W	T	F	S
		1	2	3	4	5
6	7	8	9	10	11	12
13	14	15	16	17	18	19
20	21	22	23	24	25	26
27	28	29	30			

May

S	M	T	W	T	F	S
				1	2	3
4	5	6	7	8	9	10
11	12	13	14	15	16	17
18	19	20	21	22	23	24
25	26	27	28	29	30	31

June

S	M	T	W	T	F	S
1	2	3	4	5	6	7
8	9	10	11	12	13	14
15	16	17	18	19	20	21
22	23	24	25	26	27	28
29	30					

July

S	M	T	W	T	F	S
		1	2	3	4	5
6	7	8	9	10	11	12
13	14	15	16	17	18	19
20	21	22	23	24	25	26
27	28	29	30	31		

August

S	M	T	W	T	F	S
					1	2
3	4	5	6	7	8	9
10	11	12	13	14	15	16
17	18	19	20	21	22	23
24	25	26	27	28	29	30
31						

September

S	M	T	W	T	F	S
	1	2	3	4	5	6
7	8	9	10	11	12	13
14	15	16	17	18	19	20
21	22	23	24	25	26	27
28	29	30				

October

S	M	T	W	T	F	S
			1	2	3	4
5	6	7	8	9	10	11
12	13	14	15	16	17	18
19	20	21	22	23	24	25
26	27	28	29	30	31	

November

S	M	T	W	T	F	S
						1
2	3	4	5	6	7	8
9	10	11	12	13	14	15
16	17	18	19	20	21	22
23	24	25	26	27	28	29
30						

December

S	M	T	W	T	F	S
	1	2	3	4	5	6
7	8	9	10	11	12	13
14	15	16	17	18	19	20
21	22	23	24	25	26	27
28	29	30	31			

Year in Pixels

	J	F	M	A	M	J	J	A	S	O	N	D
1.												
2.												
3.												
4.												
5.												
6.												
7.												
8.												
9.												
10.												
11.												
12.												
13.												
14.												
15.												
16.												
17.												
18.												
19.												
20.												
21.												
22.												
23.												
24.												
25.												
26.												
27.												
28.												
29.												
30.												
31.												

Color Codes

Notes

January 2025

MONDAY	TUESDAY	WEDNESDAY	THURSDAY
		1	2
6	7	8	9
13	14	15	16
20	21	22	23
27	28	29	30

January 2025

FRIDAY	SATURDAY	SUNDAY	NOTES
3	4	5	○
			○
			○
			○
			○
10	11	12	○
			○
			○
			○
17	18	19	○
			○
			○
			○
			○
24	25	26	○
			○
			○
			○
			○
31			NOTES

February 2025

MONDAY	TUESDAY	WEDNESDAY	THURSDAY
3	4	5	6
10	11	12	13
17	18	19	20
24	25	26	27

February

2025

FRIDAY	SATURDAY	SUNDAY	NOTES
	1	2	○
			○
			○
			○
			○
7	8	9	○
			○
			○
			○
			○
14	15	16	○
			○
			○
			○
21	22	23	○
			○
			○
			○
			○
28			NOTES

March 2025

MONDAY	TUESDAY	WEDNESDAY	THURSDAY
		1	2
6	7	8	9
13	14	15	16
20	21	22	23
27	28	29	30

March

2025

FRIDAY	SATURDAY	SUNDAY	NOTES
3	4	5	○
			○
			○
			○
			○
10	11	12	○
			○
			○
			○
17	18	19	○
			○
			○
			○
			○
24	25	26	○
			○
			○
			○
			○
31			NOTES

April 2025

MONDAY	TUESDAY	WEDNESDAY	THURSDAY
	1	2	3
7	8	9	10
14	15	16	17
21	22	23	24
28	29	30	

April

2025

FRIDAY	SATURDAY	SUNDAY	NOTES
4	5	6	○
			○
			○
			○
			○
11	12	13	○
			○
			○
			○
18	19	20	○
			○
			○
			○
			○
25	26	27	○
			○
			○
			○
			○
			NOTES

May 2025

MONDAY	TUESDAY	WEDNESDAY	THURSDAY
			1
5	6	7	8
12	13	14	15
19	20	21	22
26	27	28	29

May 2025

FRIDAY	SATURDAY	SUNDAY	NOTES
2	3	4	○
			○
			○
			○
			○
9	10	11	○
			○
			○
			○
16	17	18	○
			○
			○
			○
			○
23	24	25	○
			○
			○
			○
			○
30	31		NOTES

June

MONDAY	TUESDAY	WEDNESDAY	THURSDAY
2	3	4	5
9	10	11	12
16	17	18	19
23	24	25	26

June
2025

FRIDAY	SATURDAY	SUNDAY	NOTES
		1	○
			○
			○
			○
			○
6	7	8	○
			○
			○
			○
13	14	15	○
			○
			○
			○
			○
20	21	22	○
			○
			○
			○
			○
27	28	29	30

July

2025

MONDAY	TUESDAY	WEDNESDAY	THURSDAY
	1	2	3
7	8	9	10
14	15	16	17
21	22	23	24
28	29	30	31

July

2025

FRIDAY	SATURDAY	SUNDAY	NOTES
4	5	6	○
			○
			○
			○
			○
11	12	13	○
			○
			○
			○
18	19	20	○
			○
			○
			○
			○
25	26	27	○
			○
			○
			○
			○
			NOTES

August 2025

MONDAY	TUESDAY	WEDNESDAY	THURSDAY
4	5	6	7
11	12	13	14
18	19	20	21
25	26	27	28

August

2025

FRIDAY	SATURDAY	SUNDAY	NOTES
1	2	3	○
			○
			○
			○
			○
8	9	10	○
			○
			○
			○
15	16	17	○
			○
			○
			○
			○
22	23	24	NOTES
29	30	31	

September

MONDAY	TUESDAY	WEDNESDAY	THURSDAY
1	2	3	4
8	9	10	11
15	16	17	18
22	23	24	25
29	30		

September

FRIDAY	SATURDAY	SUNDAY	NOTES
5	6	7	○
			○
			○
			○
			○
12	13	14	○
			○
			○
			○
19	20	21	○
			○
			○
			○
			○
26	27	28	○
			○
			○
			○
			○
			NOTES

October

2025

MONDAY	TUESDAY	WEDNESDAY	THURSDAY
		1	2
6	7	8	9
13	14	15	16
20	21	22	23
27	28	29	30

October

2025

FRIDAY	SATURDAY	SUNDAY	NOTES
3	4	5	○
			○
			○
			○
			○
10	11	12	○
			○
			○
			○
17	18	19	○
			○
			○
			○
			○
24	25	26	○
			○
			○
			○
			○
31			NOTES

November 2025

MONDAY	TUESDAY	WEDNESDAY	THURSDAY
3	4	5	6
10	11	12	13
17	18	19	20
24	25	26	27

November

FRIDAY	SATURDAY	SUNDAY	NOTES
	1	2	○
			○
			○
			○
			○
7	8	9	○
			○
			○
			○
14	15	16	○
			○
			○
			○
			○
21	22	23	○
			○
			○
			○
			○
28	29	30	NOTES

December 2025

THURSDAY	TUESDAY	WEDNESDAY	THURSDAY
1	2	3	4
8	9	10	11
15	16	17	18
22	23	24	25
29	30	31	

December 2025

FRIDAY	SATURDAY	SUNDAY	NOTES
5	6	7	○
			○
			○
			○
			○
12	13	14	○
			○
			○
			○
19	20	21	○
			○
			○
			○
			○
26	27	28	○
			○
			○
			○
			○
			NOTES

December
2024

01 SUNDAY

○ _____
○ _____
○ _____
○ _____
○ _____
○ _____
○ _____
○ _____

02 MONDAY

○ _____
○ _____
○ _____
○ _____
○ _____
○ _____
○ _____
○ _____

03 TUESDAY

○ _____
○ _____
○ _____
○ _____
○ _____
○ _____
○ _____
○ _____

04 WEDNESDAY

○ _____
○ _____
○ _____
○ _____
○ _____

December
2024

05 THURSDAY

○ _____
○ _____
○ _____
○ _____
○ _____
○ _____
○ _____
○ _____

06 FRIDAY

○ _____
○ _____
○ _____
○ _____
○ _____
○ _____
○ _____
○ _____

07 SATURDAY

○ _____
○ _____
○ _____
○ _____
○ _____
○ _____
○ _____
○ _____

08 SUNDAY

○ _____
○ _____
○ _____
○ _____
○ _____

09 MONDAY

○ _____
○ _____
○ _____
○ _____
○ _____
○ _____
○ _____
○ _____

10 TUESDAY

○ _____
○ _____
○ _____
○ _____
○ _____
○ _____
○ _____
○ _____

11 WEDNESDAY

○ _____
○ _____
○ _____
○ _____
○ _____
○ _____
○ _____
○ _____

12 THURSDAY

○ _____
○ _____
○ _____
○ _____
○ _____

13 FRIDAY

○
○
○
○
○
○
○
○

14 SATURDAY

○
○
○
○
○
○
○
○

15 SUNDAY

○
○
○
○
○
○
○
○

16 MONDAY

○
○
○
○
○

December
2024

17 TUESDAY

○
○
○
○
○
○
○

18 WEDNESDAY

○
○
○
○
○
○
○

19 THURSDAY

○
○
○
○
○
○
○

20 FRIDAY

○
○
○
○
○

December
2024

21 SATURDAY
- ○ _____
- ○ _____
- ○ _____
- ○ _____
- ○ _____
- ○ _____
- ○ _____
- ○ _____

22 SUNDAY
- ○ _____
- ○ _____
- ○ _____
- ○ _____
- ○ _____
- ○ _____
- ○ _____
- ○ _____

23 MONDAY
- ○ _____
- ○ _____
- ○ _____
- ○ _____
- ○ _____
- ○ _____
- ○ _____
- ○ _____

24 TUESDAY
- ○ _____
- ○ _____
- ○ _____
- ○ _____
- ○ _____

25 WEDNESDAY

○
○
○
○
○
○
○
○

26 THURSDAY

○
○
○
○
○
○
○
○

27 FRIDAY

○
○
○
○
○
○
○
○

28 SATURDAY

○
○
○
○
○

29 SUNDAY

○ _____
○ _____
○ _____
○ _____
○ _____
○ _____
○ _____

30 MONDAY

○ _____
○ _____
○ _____
○ _____
○ _____
○ _____
○ _____
○ _____

31 TUESDAY

○ _____
○ _____
○ _____
○ _____
○ _____
○ _____
○ _____
○ _____

NOTES

_____
_____
_____
_____

January
2025

01 WEDNESDAY

- ○ _____
- ○ _____
- ○ _____
- ○ _____
- ○ _____
- ○ _____
- ○ _____
- ○ _____

02 THURSDAY

- ○ _____
- ○ _____
- ○ _____
- ○ _____
- ○ _____
- ○ _____
- ○ _____
- ○ _____

03 FRIDAY

- ○ _____
- ○ _____
- ○ _____
- ○ _____
- ○ _____
- ○ _____
- ○ _____
- ○ _____

04 SATURDAY

- ○ _____
- ○ _____
- ○ _____
- ○ _____
- ○ _____

January
2025

05 SUNDAY
- ○
- ○
- ○
- ○
- ○
- ○
- ○
- ○

06 MONDAY
- ○
- ○
- ○
- ○
- ○
- ○
- ○
- ○

07 TUESDAY
- ○
- ○
- ○
- ○
- ○
- ○
- ○
- ○

08 WEDNESDAY
- ○
- ○
- ○
- ○
- ○

January
2025

09 THURSDAY

○
○
○
○
○
○
○

10 FRIDAY

○
○
○
○
○
○
○

11 SATURDAY

○
○
○
○
○
○
○

12 SUNDAY

○
○
○
○
○

13 MONDAY

14 TUESDAY

15 WEDNESDAY

16 THURSDAY

17 FRIDAY

○ _____
○ _____
○ _____
○ _____
○ _____
○ _____
○ _____
○ _____

18 SATURDAY

○ _____
○ _____
○ _____
○ _____
○ _____
○ _____
○ _____
○ _____

19 SUNDAY

○ _____
○ _____
○ _____
○ _____
○ _____
○ _____
○ _____
○ _____

20 MONDAY

○ _____
○ _____
○ _____
○ _____
○ _____

21 TUESDAY

○ _____
○ _____
○ _____
○ _____
○ _____
○ _____
○ _____
○ _____

22 WEDNESDAY

○ _____
○ _____
○ _____
○ _____
○ _____
○ _____
○ _____
○ _____

23 THURSDAY

○ _____
○ _____
○ _____
○ _____
○ _____
○ _____
○ _____
○ _____

24 FRIDAY

○ _____
○ _____
○ _____
○ _____
○ _____

January
2025

25 SATURDAY

○
○
○
○
○
○
○
○

26 SUNDAY

○
○
○
○
○
○
○
○

27 MONDAY

○
○
○
○
○
○
○
○

28 TUESDAY

○
○
○
○
○

29 WEDNESDAY

○
○
○
○
○
○
○
○

30 THURSDAY

○
○
○
○
○
○
○
○

31 FRIDAY

○
○
○
○
○
○
○
○

NOTES

February
2025

01 SATURDAY

○ _____
○ _____
○ _____
○ _____
○ _____
○ _____
○ _____
○ _____

02 SUNDAY

○ _____
○ _____
○ _____
○ _____
○ _____
○ _____
○ _____
○ _____

03 MONDAY

○ _____
○ _____
○ _____
○ _____
○ _____
○ _____
○ _____
○ _____

04 TUESDAY

○ _____
○ _____
○ _____
○ _____
○ _____

05 WEDNESDAY
- ○
- ○
- ○
- ○
- ○
- ○
- ○
- ○

06 THURSDAY
- ○
- ○
- ○
- ○
- ○
- ○
- ○
- ○

07 FRIDAY
- ○
- ○
- ○
- ○
- ○
- ○
- ○
- ○

08 SATURDAY
- ○
- ○
- ○
- ○
- ○

February
2025

09 SUNDAY

10 MONDAY

11 TUESDAY

12 WEDNESDAY

February
2025

13 THURSDAY
○
○
○
○
○
○
○
○

14 FRIDAY
○
○
○
○
○
○
○
○

15 SATURDAY
○
○
○
○
○
○
○
○

16 SUNDAY
○
○
○
○
○

17 MONDAY

18 TUESDAY

19 WEDNESDAY

20 THURSDAY

February 2025

21 FRIDAY
○
○
○
○
○
○
○
○

22 SATURDAY
○
○
○
○
○
○
○
○

23 SUNDAY
○
○
○
○
○
○
○
○

24 MONDAY
○
○
○
○
○

February
2025

25 TUESDAY

26 WEDNESDAY

27 THURSDAY

28 FRIDAY

01 SATURDAY

- ○
- ○
- ○
- ○
- ○
- ○
- ○
- ○

02 SUNDAY

- ○
- ○
- ○
- ○
- ○
- ○
- ○
- ○

03 MONDAY

- ○
- ○
- ○
- ○
- ○
- ○
- ○
- ○

04 TUESDAY

- ○
- ○
- ○
- ○
- ○

05 WEDNESDAY

06 THURSDAY

07 FRIDAY

08 SATURDAY

March
2025

09 SUNDAY

10 MONDAY

11 TUESDAY

12 WEDNESDAY

March
2025

13 THURSDAY

14 FRIDAY

15 SATURDAY

16 SUNDAY

March 2025

17 MONDAY

○
○
○
○
○
○
○
○

18 TUESDAY

○
○
○
○
○
○
○
○

19 WEDNESDAY

○
○
○
○
○
○
○
○

20 THURSDAY

○
○
○
○
○

21 FRIDAY

○ _____
○ _____
○ _____
○ _____
○ _____
○ _____
○ _____
○ _____

22 SATURDAY

○ _____
○ _____
○ _____
○ _____
○ _____
○ _____
○ _____
○ _____

23 SUNDAY

○ _____
○ _____
○ _____
○ _____
○ _____
○ _____
○ _____
○ _____

24 MONDAY

○ _____
○ _____
○ _____
○ _____
○ _____

25 TUESDAY

○
○
○
○
○
○
○
○

26 WEDNESDAY

○
○
○
○
○
○
○
○

27 THURSDAY

○
○
○
○
○
○
○
○

28 FRIDAY

○
○
○
○
○

29 SATURDAY

○ _____
○ _____
○ _____
○ _____
○ _____
○ _____
○ _____
○ _____

30 SUNDAY

○ _____
○ _____
○ _____
○ _____
○ _____
○ _____
○ _____
○ _____

31 MONDAY

○ _____
○ _____
○ _____
○ _____
○ _____
○ _____
○ _____
○ _____

NOTES

_____
_____
_____
_____

01 TUESDAY

○
○
○
○
○
○
○
○

02 WEDNESDAY

○
○
○
○
○
○
○
○

03 THURSDAY

○
○
○
○
○
○
○
○

04 FRIDAY

○
○
○
○
○

05 SATURDAY

○ _____
○ _____
○ _____
○ _____
○ _____
○ _____
○ _____
○ _____

06 SUNDAY

○ _____
○ _____
○ _____
○ _____
○ _____
○ _____
○ _____
○ _____

07 MONDAY

○ _____
○ _____
○ _____
○ _____
○ _____
○ _____
○ _____
○ _____

08 TUESDAY

○ _____
○ _____
○ _____
○ _____
○ _____

09 WEDNESDAY

○ _____
○ _____
○ _____
○ _____
○ _____
○ _____
○ _____
○ _____

10 THURSDAY

○ _____
○ _____
○ _____
○ _____
○ _____
○ _____
○ _____
○ _____

11 FRIDAY

○ _____
○ _____
○ _____
○ _____
○ _____
○ _____
○ _____
○ _____

12 SATURDAY

○ _____
○ _____
○ _____
○ _____
○ _____

April
2025

13 SUNDAY

○
○
○
○
○
○
○

14 MONDAY

○
○
○
○
○
○
○
○

15 TUESDAY

○
○
○
○
○
○
○
○

16 WEDNESDAY

○
○
○
○
○

17 THURSDAY

○ _____
○ _____
○ _____
○ _____
○ _____
○ _____
○ _____
○ _____

18 FRIDAY

○ _____
○ _____
○ _____
○ _____
○ _____
○ _____
○ _____
○ _____

19 SATURDAY

○ _____
○ _____
○ _____
○ _____
○ _____
○ _____
○ _____
○ _____

20 SUNDAY

○ _____
○ _____
○ _____
○ _____
○ _____

21 MONDAY

○ _____
○ _____
○ _____
○ _____
○ _____
○ _____
○ _____
○ _____

22 TUESDAY

○ _____
○ _____
○ _____
○ _____
○ _____
○ _____
○ _____
○ _____

23 WEDNESDAY

○ _____
○ _____
○ _____
○ _____
○ _____
○ _____
○ _____
○ _____

24 THURSDAY

○ _____
○ _____
○ _____
○ _____
○ _____

25 FRIDAY

○ _____
○ _____
○ _____
○ _____
○ _____
○ _____
○ _____
○ _____

26 SATURDAY

○ _____
○ _____
○ _____
○ _____
○ _____
○ _____
○ _____
○ _____

27 SUNDAY

○ _____
○ _____
○ _____
○ _____
○ _____
○ _____
○ _____
○ _____

28 MONDAY

○ _____
○ _____
○ _____
○ _____
○ _____

29 TUESDAY

○ _____
○ _____
○ _____
○ _____
○ _____
○ _____
○ _____
○ _____

30 WEDNESDAY

○ _____
○ _____
○ _____
○ _____
○ _____
○ _____
○ _____
○ _____

NOTES

_____
_____
_____
_____
_____
_____
_____
_____
_____
_____
_____
_____
_____

May
2025

01 THURSDAY
○
○
○
○
○
○
○
○

02 FRIDAY
○
○
○
○
○
○
○
○

03 SATURDAY
○
○
○
○
○
○
○
○

04 SUNDAY
○
○
○
○
○

May
2025

05 MONDAY

○ _____
○ _____
○ _____
○ _____
○ _____
○ _____
○ _____
○ _____

06 TUESDAY

○ _____
○ _____
○ _____
○ _____
○ _____
○ _____
○ _____
○ _____

07 WEDNESDAY

○ _____
○ _____
○ _____
○ _____
○ _____
○ _____
○ _____
○ _____

08 THURSDAY

○ _____
○ _____
○ _____
○ _____
○ _____

May
2025

09 FRIDAY
○
○
○
○
○
○
○
○

10 SATURDAY
○
○
○
○
○
○
○
○

11 SUNDAY
○
○
○
○
○
○
○
○

12 MONDAY
○
○
○
○
○

May
2025

13 TUESDAY

○ _____
○ _____
○ _____
○ _____
○ _____
○ _____
○ _____
○ _____

14 WEDNESDAY

○ _____
○ _____
○ _____
○ _____
○ _____
○ _____
○ _____
○ _____

15 THURSDAY

○ _____
○ _____
○ _____
○ _____
○ _____
○ _____
○ _____
○ _____

16 FRIDAY

○ _____
○ _____
○ _____
○ _____
○ _____

17 SATURDAY

○
○
○
○
○
○
○
○

18 SUNDAY

○
○
○
○
○
○
○
○

19 MONDAY

○
○
○
○
○
○
○
○

20 TUESDAY

○
○
○
○
○

21 WEDNESDAY

22 THURSDAY

23 FRIDAY

24 SATURDAY

25 SUNDAY

○ _____
○ _____
○ _____
○ _____
○ _____
○ _____
○ _____
○ _____

26 MONDAY

○ _____
○ _____
○ _____
○ _____
○ _____
○ _____
○ _____
○ _____

27 TUESDAY

○ _____
○ _____
○ _____
○ _____
○ _____
○ _____
○ _____
○ _____

28 WEDNESDAY

○ _____
○ _____
○ _____
○ _____
○ _____

May
2025

29 THURSDAY

○
○
○
○
○
○
○
○

30 FRIDAY

○
○
○
○
○
○
○
○

31 SATURDAY

○
○
○
○
○
○
○
○

NOTES

June 2025

01 SUNDAY

○ _____
○ _____
○ _____
○ _____
○ _____
○ _____
○ _____
○ _____

02 MONDAY

○ _____
○ _____
○ _____
○ _____
○ _____
○ _____
○ _____
○ _____

03 TUESDAY

○ _____
○ _____
○ _____
○ _____
○ _____
○ _____
○ _____
○ _____

04 WEDNESDAY

○ _____
○ _____
○ _____
○ _____
○ _____

June 2025

05 THURSDAY

○ _____
○ _____
○ _____
○ _____
○ _____
○ _____
○ _____
○ _____

06 FRIDAY

○ _____
○ _____
○ _____
○ _____
○ _____
○ _____
○ _____
○ _____

07 SATURDAY

○ _____
○ _____
○ _____
○ _____
○ _____
○ _____
○ _____
○ _____

08 SUNDAY

○ _____
○ _____
○ _____
○ _____
○ _____

June 2025

09 MONDAY
○ _____
○ _____
○ _____
○ _____
○ _____
○ _____
○ _____
○ _____

10 TUESDAY
○ _____
○ _____
○ _____
○ _____
○ _____
○ _____
○ _____
○ _____

11 WEDNESDAY
○ _____
○ _____
○ _____
○ _____
○ _____
○ _____
○ _____
○ _____

12 THURSDAY
○ _____
○ _____
○ _____
○ _____
○ _____

13 FRIDAY

○
○
○
○
○
○
○

14 SATURDAY

○
○
○
○
○
○
○
○

15 SUNDAY

○
○
○
○
○
○
○
○

16 MONDAY

○
○
○
○
○

17 TUESDAY

○
○
○
○
○
○
○
○

18 WEDNESDAY

○
○
○
○
○
○
○
○

19 THURSDAY

○
○
○
○
○
○
○
○

20 FRIDAY

○
○
○
○
○

21 SATURDAY
- ○ _____
- ○ _____
- ○ _____
- ○ _____
- ○ _____
- ○ _____
- ○ _____
- ○ _____

22 SUNDAY
- ○ _____
- ○ _____
- ○ _____
- ○ _____
- ○ _____
- ○ _____
- ○ _____
- ○ _____

23 MONDAY
- ○ _____
- ○ _____
- ○ _____
- ○ _____
- ○ _____
- ○ _____
- ○ _____
- ○ _____

24 TUESDAY
- ○ _____
- ○ _____
- ○ _____
- ○ _____
- ○ _____

25 WEDNESDAY

○ _____
○ _____
○ _____
○ _____
○ _____
○ _____
○ _____
○ _____

26 THURSDAY

○ _____
○ _____
○ _____
○ _____
○ _____
○ _____
○ _____
○ _____

27 FRIDAY

○ _____
○ _____
○ _____
○ _____
○ _____
○ _____
○ _____
○ _____

28 SATURDAY

○ _____
○ _____
○ _____
○ _____
○ _____

29 SUNDAY

○ _____
○ _____
○ _____
○ _____
○ _____
○ _____
○ _____
○ _____

30 MONDAY

○ _____
○ _____
○ _____
○ _____
○ _____
○ _____
○ _____
○ _____

NOTES

_____
_____
_____
_____
_____
_____
_____
_____
_____
_____
_____

July
2025

01 TUESDAY

○ _____
○ _____
○ _____
○ _____
○ _____
○ _____
○ _____
○ _____

02 WEDNESDAY

○ _____
○ _____
○ _____
○ _____
○ _____
○ _____
○ _____
○ _____

03 THURSDAY

○ _____
○ _____
○ _____
○ _____
○ _____
○ _____
○ _____
○ _____

04 FRIDAY

○ _____
○ _____
○ _____
○ _____
○ _____

July
2025

05 SATURDAY

○
○
○
○
○
○
○

06 SUNDAY

○
○
○
○
○
○
○
○

07 MONDAY

○
○
○
○
○
○
○
○

08 TUESDAY

○
○
○
○
○

09 WEDNESDAY

○
○
○
○
○
○
○
○

10 THURSDAY

○
○
○
○
○
○
○
○

11 FRIDAY

○
○
○
○
○
○
○
○

12 SATURDAY

○
○
○
○
○

13 SUNDAY

○
○
○
○
○
○
○

14 MONDAY

○
○
○
○
○
○
○
○

15 TUESDAY

○
○
○
○
○
○
○
○

16 WEDNESDAY

○
○
○
○
○

17 THURSDAY

○
○
○
○
○
○
○
○

18 FRIDAY

○
○
○
○
○
○
○
○
○

19 SATURDAY

○
○
○
○
○
○
○
○

20 SUNDAY

○
○
○
○
○

July
2025

21 MONDAY

○ _____
○ _____
○ _____
○ _____
○ _____
○ _____
○ _____
○ _____

22 TUESDAY

○ _____
○ _____
○ _____
○ _____
○ _____
○ _____
○ _____
○ _____

23 WEDNESDAY

○ _____
○ _____
○ _____
○ _____
○ _____
○ _____
○ _____
○ _____

24 THURSDAY

○ _____
○ _____
○ _____
○ _____
○ _____

July
2025

25 FRIDAY
○
○
○
○
○
○
○
○

26 SATURDAY
○
○
○
○
○
○
○
○
○

27 SUNDAY
○
○
○
○
○
○
○
○

28 MONDAY
○
○
○
○
○

July
2025

29 TUESDAY

○ _____
○ _____
○ _____
○ _____
○ _____
○ _____
○ _____
○ _____

30 WEDNESDAY

○ _____
○ _____
○ _____
○ _____
○ _____
○ _____
○ _____
○ _____

31 THURSDAY

○ _____
○ _____
○ _____
○ _____
○ _____
○ _____
○ _____
○ _____

NOTES

_____
_____
_____
_____

August
2025

01 FRIDAY
- ○
- ○
- ○
- ○
- ○
- ○
- ○
- ○

02 SATURDAY
- ○
- ○
- ○
- ○
- ○
- ○
- ○
- ○

03 SUNDAY
- ○
- ○
- ○
- ○
- ○
- ○
- ○
- ○

04 MONDAY
- ○
- ○
- ○
- ○
- ○

05 TUESDAY

○ _____
○ _____
○ _____
○ _____
○ _____
○ _____
○ _____
○ _____

06 WEDNESDAY

○ _____
○ _____
○ _____
○ _____
○ _____
○ _____
○ _____
○ _____

07 THURSDAY

○ _____
○ _____
○ _____
○ _____
○ _____
○ _____
○ _____
○ _____

08 FRIDAY

○ _____
○ _____
○ _____
○ _____
○ _____

09 SATURDAY

10 SUNDAY

11 MONDAY

12 TUESDAY

13 WEDNESDAY

14 THURSDAY

15 FRIDAY

16 SATURDAY

17 SUNDAY

18 MONDAY

19 TUESDAY

20 WEDNESDAY

21 THURSDAY

- ○
- ○
- ○
- ○
- ○
- ○
- ○
- ○

22 FRIDAY

- ○
- ○
- ○
- ○
- ○
- ○
- ○
- ○

23 SATURDAY

- ○
- ○
- ○
- ○
- ○
- ○
- ○
- ○

24 SUNDAY

- ○
- ○
- ○
- ○
- ○

25 MONDAY

○
○
○
○
○
○
○
○

26 TUESDAY

○
○
○
○
○
○
○
○

27 WEDNESDAY

○
○
○
○
○
○
○
○

28 THURSDAY

○
○
○
○
○

29 FRIDAY

○ _____
○ _____
○ _____
○ _____
○ _____
○ _____
○ _____
○ _____

30 SATURDAY

○ _____
○ _____
○ _____
○ _____
○ _____
○ _____
○ _____
○ _____

31 SUNDAY

○ _____
○ _____
○ _____
○ _____
○ _____
○ _____
○ _____
○ _____

NOTES

_____
_____
_____
_____

01 MONDAY

○ _____
○ _____
○ _____
○ _____
○ _____
○ _____
○ _____
○ _____

02 TUESDAY

○ _____
○ _____
○ _____
○ _____
○ _____
○ _____
○ _____
○ _____

03 WEDNESDAY

○ _____
○ _____
○ _____
○ _____
○ _____
○ _____
○ _____
○ _____

04 THURSDAY

○ _____
○ _____
○ _____
○ _____
○ _____

September
2025

05 FRIDAY

○ _____
○ _____
○ _____
○ _____
○ _____
○ _____
○ _____
○ _____

06 SATURDAY

○ _____
○ _____
○ _____
○ _____
○ _____
○ _____
○ _____
○ _____

07 SUNDAY

○ _____
○ _____
○ _____
○ _____
○ _____
○ _____
○ _____
○ _____

08 MONDAY

○ _____
○ _____
○ _____
○ _____
○ _____

09 TUESDAY

○ _____
○ _____
○ _____
○ _____
○ _____
○ _____
○ _____
○ _____

10 WEDNESDAY

○ _____
○ _____
○ _____
○ _____
○ _____
○ _____
○ _____
○ _____

11 THURSDAY

○ _____
○ _____
○ _____
○ _____
○ _____
○ _____
○ _____
○ _____

12 FRIDAY

○ _____
○ _____
○ _____
○ _____
○ _____

13 SATURDAY

○
○
○
○
○
○
○
○

14 SUNDAY

○
○
○
○
○
○
○
○

15 MONDAY

○
○
○
○
○
○
○
○

16 TUESDAY

○
○
○
○
○

17 WEDNESDAY

○
○
○
○
○
○
○
○

18 THURSDAY

○
○
○
○
○
○
○
○

19 FRIDAY

○
○
○
○
○
○
○
○

20 SATURDAY

○
○
○
○
○

21 SUNDAY

○
○
○
○
○
○
○
○

22 MONDAY

○
○
○
○
○
○
○
○

23 TUESDAY

○
○
○
○
○
○
○
○

24 WEDNESDAY

○
○
○
○
○

25 THURSDAY

○ _____
○ _____
○ _____
○ _____
○ _____
○ _____
○ _____
○ _____

26 FRIDAY

○ _____
○ _____
○ _____
○ _____
○ _____
○ _____
○ _____
○ _____

27 SATURDAY

○ _____
○ _____
○ _____
○ _____
○ _____
○ _____
○ _____
○ _____

28 SUNDAY

○ _____
○ _____
○ _____
○ _____
○ _____

September
2025

29 MONDAY

- ○ _____
- ○ _____
- ○ _____
- ○ _____
- ○ _____
- ○ _____
- ○ _____
- ○ _____

30 TUESDAY

- ○ _____
- ○ _____
- ○ _____
- ○ _____
- ○ _____
- ○ _____
- ○ _____
- ○ _____

NOTES

_____
_____
_____
_____
_____
_____
_____
_____
_____
_____
_____

October
2025

01 WEDNESDAY
- ○
- ○
- ○
- ○
- ○
- ○
- ○
- ○

02 THURSDAY
- ○
- ○
- ○
- ○
- ○
- ○
- ○
- ○

03 FRIDAY
- ○
- ○
- ○
- ○
- ○
- ○
- ○
- ○

04 SATURDAY
- ○
- ○
- ○
- ○
- ○

October
2025

05 SUNDAY

○ _____
○ _____
○ _____
○ _____
○ _____
○ _____
○ _____
○ _____

06 MONDAY

○ _____
○ _____
○ _____
○ _____
○ _____
○ _____
○ _____
○ _____

07 TUESDAY

○ _____
○ _____
○ _____
○ _____
○ _____
○ _____
○ _____
○ _____

08 WEDNESDAY

○ _____
○ _____
○ _____
○ _____
○ _____

09 THURSDAY

○
○
○
○
○
○
○
○

10 FRIDAY

○
○
○
○
○
○
○
○

11 SATURDAY

○
○
○
○
○
○
○
○

12 SUNDAY

○
○
○
○
○

13 MONDAY

- ○ ....
- ○ ....
- ○ ....
- ○ ....
- ○ ....
- ○ ....
- ○ ....
- ○ ....

14 TUESDAY

- ○ ....
- ○ ....
- ○ ....
- ○ ....
- ○ ....
- ○ ....
- ○ ....
- ○ ....

15 WEDNESDAY

- ○ ....
- ○ ....
- ○ ....
- ○ ....
- ○ ....
- ○ ....
- ○ ....
- ○ ....

16 THURSDAY

- ○ ....
- ○ ....
- ○ ....
- ○ ....
- ○ ....

17 FRIDAY

○
○
○
○
○
○
○
○

18 SATURDAY

○
○
○
○
○
○
○
○

19 SUNDAY

○
○
○
○
○
○
○
○

20 MONDAY

○
○
○
○
○

October
2025

21 TUESDAY
○
○
○
○
○
○
○
○

22 WEDNESDAY
○
○
○
○
○
○
○
○

23 THURSDAY
○
○
○
○
○
○
○
○

24 FRIDAY
○
○
○
○
○

25 SATURDAY

○
○
○
○
○
○
○
○

26 SUNDAY

○
○
○
○
○
○
○
○

27 MONDAY

○
○
○
○
○
○
○
○

28 TUESDAY

○
○
○
○
○

29 WEDNESDAY

- ○ _____
- ○ _____
- ○ _____
- ○ _____
- ○ _____
- ○ _____
- ○ _____
- ○ _____

30 THURSDAY

- ○ _____
- ○ _____
- ○ _____
- ○ _____
- ○ _____
- ○ _____
- ○ _____
- ○ _____

31 FRIDAY

- ○ _____
- ○ _____
- ○ _____
- ○ _____
- ○ _____
- ○ _____
- ○ _____
- ○ _____

NOTES

_____
_____
_____
_____

November
2025

01 SATURDAY
○
○
○
○
○
○
○
○

02 SUNDAY
○
○
○
○
○
○
○
○

03 MONDAY
○
○
○
○
○
○
○
○

04 TUESDAY
○
○
○
○
○

November
2025

05 WEDNESDAY

○ _____
○ _____
○ _____
○ _____
○ _____
○ _____
○ _____
○ _____

06 THURSDAY

○ _____
○ _____
○ _____
○ _____
○ _____
○ _____
○ _____
○ _____

07 FRIDAY

○ _____
○ _____
○ _____
○ _____
○ _____
○ _____
○ _____
○ _____

08 SATURDAY

○ _____
○ _____
○ _____
○ _____
○ _____

November
2025

09 SUNDAY

○ _____
○ _____
○ _____
○ _____
○ _____
○ _____
○ _____
○ _____

10 MONDAY

○ _____
○ _____
○ _____
○ _____
○ _____
○ _____
○ _____
○ _____

11 TUESDAY

○ _____
○ _____
○ _____
○ _____
○ _____
○ _____
○ _____
○ _____

12 WEDNESDAY

○ _____
○ _____
○ _____
○ _____
○ _____

13 THURSDAY

14 FRIDAY

15 SATURDAY

16 SUNDAY

17 MONDAY

○
○
○
○
○
○
○
○

18 TUESDAY

○
○
○
○
○
○
○
○
○

19 WEDNESDAY

○
○
○
○
○
○
○
○

20 THURSDAY

○
○
○
○
○

21 FRIDAY

○ _____
○ _____
○ _____
○ _____
○ _____
○ _____
○ _____
○ _____

22 SATURDAY

○ _____
○ _____
○ _____
○ _____
○ _____
○ _____
○ _____
○ _____

23 SUNDAY

○ _____
○ _____
○ _____
○ _____
○ _____
○ _____
○ _____
○ _____

24 MONDAY

○ _____
○ _____
○ _____
○ _____
○ _____

November
2025

25 TUESDAY

○
○
○
○
○
○
○
○

26 WEDNESDAY

○
○
○
○
○
○
○
○
○

27 THURSDAY

○
○
○
○
○
○
○
○

28 FRIDAY

○
○
○
○
○

29 SATURDAY

- ○
- ○
- ○
- ○
- ○
- ○
- ○
- ○

30 SUNDAY

- ○
- ○
- ○
- ○
- ○
- ○
- ○
- ○

NOTES

December
2025

01 MONDAY
○
○
○
○
○
○
○
○

02 TUESDAY
○
○
○
○
○
○
○
○

03 WEDNESDAY
○
○
○
○
○
○
○
○

04 THURSDAY
○
○
○
○
○

December
2025

05 FRIDAY

- ○ _____
- ○ _____
- ○ _____
- ○ _____
- ○ _____
- ○ _____
- ○ _____
- ○ _____

06 SATURDAY

- ○ _____
- ○ _____
- ○ _____
- ○ _____
- ○ _____
- ○ _____
- ○ _____
- ○ _____

07 SUNDAY

- ○ _____
- ○ _____
- ○ _____
- ○ _____
- ○ _____
- ○ _____
- ○ _____
- ○ _____

08 MONDAY

- ○ _____
- ○ _____
- ○ _____
- ○ _____
- ○ _____

December
2025

09 TUESDAY
○
○
○
○
○
○
○
○

10 WEDNESDAY
○
○
○
○
○
○
○
○

11 THURSDAY
○
○
○
○
○
○
○
○

12 FRIDAY
○
○
○
○
○

13 SATURDAY

○
○
○
○
○
○
○
○

14 SUNDAY

○
○
○
○
○
○
○
○

15 MONDAY

○
○
○
○
○
○
○
○

16 TUESDAY

○
○
○
○
○

17 WEDNESDAY

○ _____
○ _____
○ _____
○ _____
○ _____
○ _____
○ _____
○ _____

18 THURSDAY

○ _____
○ _____
○ _____
○ _____
○ _____
○ _____
○ _____
○ _____
○ _____

19 FRIDAY

○ _____
○ _____
○ _____
○ _____
○ _____
○ _____
○ _____
○ _____

20 SATURDAY

○ _____
○ _____
○ _____
○ _____
○ _____

December
2025

21 SUNDAY
- ○
- ○
- ○
- ○
- ○
- ○
- ○

22 MONDAY
- ○
- ○
- ○
- ○
- ○
- ○
- ○
- ○

23 TUESDAY
- ○
- ○
- ○
- ○
- ○
- ○
- ○
- ○

24 WEDNESDAY
- ○
- ○
- ○
- ○
- ○

December
2025

25 THURSDAY

○
○
○
○
○
○
○
○

26 FRIDAY

○
○
○
○
○
○
○
○

27 SATURDAY

○
○
○
○
○
○
○
○

28 SUNDAY

○
○
○
○
○

December
2025

29 MONDAY

- ○ _____
- ○ _____
- ○ _____
- ○ _____
- ○ _____
- ○ _____
- ○ _____
- ○ _____

30 TUESDAY

- ○ _____
- ○ _____
- ○ _____
- ○ _____
- ○ _____
- ○ _____
- ○ _____
- ○ _____

31 WEDNESDAY

- ○ _____
- ○ _____
- ○ _____
- ○ _____
- ○ _____
- ○ _____
- ○ _____
- ○ _____

NOTES

_____
_____
_____
_____

www.ingramcontent.com/pod-product-compliance
Lightning Source LLC
Chambersburg PA
CBHW052115020426
42335CB00021B/2768